d word from a

e call from a

int it kind

e lights the way

believe there are

own to us from

me to you and

us how to li

e us with the

ear so many fo

To my own Angel—

Diane – 12-25-98

Love,
Don

ISBN 0-373-15288-4

ANGELS AMONG US

Edited by Laura Shin
Art Direction by Shelley Cinnamon
Designed by John Kicksee & Tara Kelly
Special Thanks and Acknowledgement to Tracy Nesdoly

Printed in U.S.A.

FIRST EDITION

ALABAMA

Angels AMONG US

HARLEQUIN®

TORONTO • NEW YORK • LONDON
AMSTERDAM • PARIS • SYDNEY • HAMBURG
STOCKHOLM • ATHENS • TOKYO • MILAN • MADRID
PRAGUE • WARSAW • BUDAPEST • AUCKLAND

Angels Among Us

I WAS WALKING HOME FROM SCHOOL ON A COLD WINTER DAY
TOOK A SHORTCUT THROUGH THE WOODS, AND I LOST MY WAY
IT WAS GETTIN' LATE, AND I WAS SCARED AND ALONE
BUT THEN A KIND OLD MAN TOOK MY HAND AND LED ME HOME
NOW MAMA COULDN'T SEE HIM OH BUT HE WAS STANDING THERE
AND I KNEW IN MY HEART HE WAS THE ANSWER TO MY PRAYER

OH I BELIEVE THERE ARE ANGELS AMONG US
SENT DOWN TO US FROM SOMEWHERE UP ABOVE
THEY COME TO YOU AND ME IN OUR DARKEST HOURS
TO SHOW US HOW TO LIVE, TO TEACH US HOW TO GIVE
TO GUIDE US WITH THE LIGHT OF LOVE

WHEN LIFE HELD TROUBLED TIMES AND HAD ME DOWN ON MY KNEES
THERE'S ALWAYS BEEN SOMEONE TO COME ALONG AND COMFORT ME
A KIND WORD FROM A STRANGER TO LEND A HELPING HAND
A PHONE CALL FROM A FRIEND JUST TO SAY I UNDERSTAND
NOW AIN'T IT KIND OF FUNNY, AT THE DARK END OF THE ROAD
SOMEONE LIGHTS THE WAY WITH JUST A SINGLE RAY OF HOPE

THEY WEAR SO MANY FACES
SHOW UP IN THE STRANGEST PLACES
TO GRACE US WITH THEIR MERCY IN OUR TIME OF NEED

—Don Goodman & Becky Hobbs

When I heard "Angels Among Us," I realized it was a very powerful song. But I really didn't know what to do about recording it. It was totally different and though I've always been one who liked to do songs that were different, I wasn't sure. So the song kind of lay around for a few weeks.

But my three-year-old daughter, Randa, heard the song, and she just loved it. At that time, of course, she was too young to really know how to operate the cassette player, so I'd play it for her. And then one weekend my oldest daughter's friend, Jacey Colburn, was killed in a car accident.

My wife and my children are very close to her family, and Randa felt a very strong attachment to Jacey because Jacey had played with her when she was little. To her that was just something real special.

One day, Randa and I were sitting on the couch, and she wanted me to play the song "Angels" again. She said "Daddy, you have to do that song—because that's Jacey's song." "Angels" was a song her daddy could sing that would make things better. At the time, I wondered if I could write a song or something that maybe would help the family. Little did I know that all along the answer was right there.

Unfortunately, it wasn't well received by the producer or the record company we were working with at the time. They didn't think it was a song Alabama should do.

But I kept hearing that little three-year-old's voice saying, "Daddy, you've got to do this song for Jacey." One day I was sitting on the couch with her again, when she asked to hear the song. I played it for her, and she said, "Daddy, what are the words to that song?" So I just started saying the words, "I was walking home from school on a cold winter day, took a shortcut through the woods, and I lost my way. It was getting late...." As I did that, she snuggled up closer to me and got hold of my hand, and I realized then that was the approach to take . That was how "Angels" had to be done.

Still the song would have never gotten on the CD had it not been for my bandmate, Teddy Gentry. Teddy told everyone that if it meant that much to me, if I believed in it that much, then the song that he'd recorded could be taken off the CD to make room for "Angels."

What happened next was purely magical, spiritual. The song took on a life of its own. There was little promotion behind it. When people heard the song they cried or they shouted or they wept for joy. They wanted to know where they could go to buy that record. It was just a very special, special thing.

Not only was it special for me, but it let me say things and touch people who were down and out on their luck. It gave me the opportunity to reach people in an uplifting way, which I had never before been able to do as a part of Alabama. And, incredibly, the people who heard the song let us know how much "Angels" meant to them. We received letters and e-mails, and everywhere we went strangers would tell us their stories. One of the song's greatest legacies is that it moves a cross section of people: Black, White, Hispanic. Every person in the world is touched by this song.

I have to say that I'm proud I listened to my little girl. All this was done because of the simple spirit of a little child. And I think that's really why this song works. It goes straight to the heart and spirit of every person, every being, young and old alike.

—Randy Owen
ALABAMA

My mom and dad divorced early on. So as a young boy I went to live with my mom's father in DeKalb County, Alabama. My grandpa was a very special man. As I was growing up he became a lot more than just someone who I lived with—more even than just a grandpa. I think he taught me about having unconditional love for your family—that no matter what, love is always love—which I try to carry through to my kids today. I think that love is missing from too many families today. My grandpa taught me right from wrong and was always the shoulder I leaned on and the rock I clung to growing up. He gave me the basics for life and showed me kindness.

He was my guardian angel, as far as someone who was put here to make a difference in my life. In my eyes he made all the difference in the world. He showed me how to stand on my own and to try and be a good person. I know that even though he passed away some time back he still watches over me. I can feel his spirit and his warmth especially in the old homeplace on Lookout Mountain. Burt Eller was a good man and I'm sure is an even better angel. Thanks, Paw Paw.

— Teddy Gentry
ALABAMA

Angels? When I was asked to write about an angel in my life, I really had to give it some thought. I guess, looking back, there have been many angels in my life even though at the time, I didn't think of them that way.

Just to spotlight a few, my grandparents, J. Herbert and Rhoda Cook, who lived next door to me. They encouraged my music pursuits even though they worked in a sock mill for as long as I can remember and weren't by any means wealthy. They seemed to always find a way to help me get instruments.

My parents were and still are angels to me. I think of how I was taught things by both of them. My mother has met so many of our fans, and it seems I have had countless comments from fans all over the country who have come to the June Jams and have been impressed by her kindness and outgoing personality. I remember in grade school, every classroom would have two or three room mothers, who would bring cookies and Kool-Aid to certain occasions. I always enjoyed having my mom as a room mother because she seemed to enjoy doing it and, of course, I thought my mom was prettier than all the other kids' moms. My dad has always been a source of knowledge and strength to me, even if he wasn't aware of it, teaching me everything from my first guitar chords to how to fish. I could fill a book if I started sorting through my memories....

A lot of people, especially kids, seem to have been put here for a short time and have touched the lives of others. I think they must be angels with a purpose. We have met many of them during our years with Alabama.

Lastly, I've found my own special angel—my Sweetest of Hearts, Lisa.

—Jeff Cook
ALABAMA

9

A Note from Mark Herndon

As I sit here thinking about what to write, it occurs to me to ask, "What is my situation right now?" At this moment I'm sitting in a hospital emergency room where my father is having major surgery. He's already been there for about seven hours. His future is in the hands of God, of course, and the surgeons.

I've never seen my father down and out. He's an extremely strong and honorable man who fought in World War II, Korea and Vietnam. I always thought him somewhat invincible.

About an hour or so into the operation a member of the hospital staff placed some magazines around the room for those of us hoping to pass the time here a little more quickly. On the stack placed next to me was an issue of *PEOPLE* magazine featuring real-life stories of angels. Now I have to admit after twenty-some years in the music business I am something of a skeptic. But, as I read some of the tales told, I began to feel very calm about the outcome of this day's events. There was almost an audible, "Not here, not today, don't worry" kind of reassurance. It eased my mind for the next six hours or so.

I could also tell you some stories. Like the time—29,000 feet over Washington, D.C.—I had to help bring a very sick airplane into Dulles Airport and knew not only that I was going to make it, but everything I had to do. As though someone with far greater experience than me was right there coaching me through.

Or, the time while riding a bike on a residential street I stopped cold for no reason at all. In the next instant, a speeding car ran the stop sign at what would have been the same moment I was crossing the intersection.

Or, the time on I-75. Or... My point is: there are angels among us and they help us navigate life's treacherous waters daily. All you have to do is look around the room like I did today. They might be closer than you think.

By the way, Dad is doing great.

—*Mark Herndon*
ALABAMA

Shortly before Christmas 1985, I started getting premonitions that I was going to be in a bad vehicle accident. They would happen to me as I was drifting off to sleep. All of a sudden, I'd sit up in bed, my heart pounding, with an overwhelming feeling of despair, a very sickening feeling. This feeling persisted, and then on January 24, 1986, in the wee hours of the morning, something very weird happened.

I was in my kitchen, making a cake—chocolate, of course—for a gathering that I was having later that day to celebrate my birthday. As I was stirring the batter, "something" took hold of my elbow and was urging me to go outside. I wasn't really scared, but I felt extremely uneasy—like when you're getting ready to hear something you don't want to hear. I stood out in the front yard, looked up at the starry sky, and asked out loud, "What? What is it you're trying to tell me?" And this loud, very strong, masculine voice said, *"Be careful. This may be your last birthday!"* I got the same sick feeling of despair that I got when I was having those premonitions. I just stood there, dumbfounded, asking out loud for more information, but that was all I was given. I knew I was being warned about something, and I had a pretty good idea that it was connected to those premonitions.

I went back in the house. My knees were shaking and my heart was pounding. My mind kept going over every word. "Be careful. This *may* be your last birthday." *May* was the key word. It must have been something I could prevent. Otherwise, why was I being warned? And *who* was warning me? At the time, I thought it was God, or my sweet, loving Daddy (with a deeper voice), who passed away in 1982.

The next day, January 25, 1986, my band and I had just performed at a police benefit in Albertville, Alabama. We were stopped at a traffic light at a highway intersection, and it was raining. I was sitting in the back of the van, on the left. Randy, our road manager, was driving. I looked out the window and saw an eighteen-wheeler barreling toward the intersection. I thought, "My God, if his light turns red, he's not going to be able to stop!" I then looked up, and our light turned green. In what must have been a moment—but seemed like forever—I felt Randy lift his foot off the brake and the van start moving forward, and I got that same sick feeling. I yelled *"Stop!"* I knew that Randy didn't see the truck, but he stepped on the brakes just as the eighteen-wheeler, blowing his air horn, slammed into us. He hit the front left side of my Dodge Maxi Van—fortunately the strongest part. Our equipment-packed trailer was knocked off, and we slid around on the wet pavement. The van was totaled, but we were alive. If Randy had stopped a split second later, we would have been broadsided and, from what the police officers told us, most likely killed.

It took a lot of thinking and some time for me to realize the voice I'd heard was that of my Guardian Angel. I wrote down the title "Angels Among Us" in my notebook, and savored it for years. I had the chorus started and a good melody going. A few years later, I saw the movie, *Fried Green Tomatoes*. In it Jessica Tandy says something like, "I do believe there are angels among us." I got goose bumps and knew that it was a sign for me to finish the song. I went home and worked on the song all night long. But it *still* wasn't finished.

Then came Christmas, 1992. I was visiting my mom in Oklahoma. Once again, it was the wee hours of the morning—my favorite time—and I was sitting in my dad's easy chair. I got the strongest feeling that I *had* to finish the song. But for some odd reason, it wasn't "coming". I have written songs long enough to know you have to let them come. If you force a song, it sounds like it.

In January, when I got back home to Nashville, I called Don Goodman. Don is a great songwriter, and we've written a lot of good songs together through the years. When I played what I had of the song for him, he felt the power, and tears came to his eyes. We wanted to write it so children could understand it. That's why we wrote the first verse about walking home from school. It took us a couple of sessions to finish it, but we knew we had something special to share with others.

Maybe writing this song was one of the reasons I wasn't taken on January 25, 1986. I hope there are more. Lots more!

—Becky Hobbs
songwriter, "Angels Among Us"

In January of 1993, my sixteen-year-old son was involved in an automobile accident and two of his close friends were killed. We were devastated. I don't know how we would have coped with the tragedy if not for the countless phone calls and letters from family, friends and total strangers who read about it in the paper and called to tell us we were in their prayers. This was where my thoughts and feelings were when Becky called me and asked me to help her write "Angels Among Us." Every word came from the heart....

"When life held troubled times and had me down on my knees, there's always been someone to come along and comfort me. A kind word from a stranger to lend a helping hand, a phone call from a friend just to say they understand."

Becky and I talked about our lives and all the angels both real and celestial who have always been there for us. We talked about our years in Nashville trying to make a go as songwriters and all the times our backs were against the wall and we didn't know how we were going to keep our dreams alive but somehow, someway there was always an angel....

"Now ain't it kinda funny at the dark end of the road, how someone lights the way with just a single ray of hope."

This song has been used by the Red Cross, United Way, Special Olympics, children's hospitals, nursing homes, firefighters, emergency medical services, at funerals, weddings and schools, just to name a few. And almost every day we receive letters telling us how "Angels Among Us" has helped someone else. Maybe angels helped us write it.

Oh yes, I believe there are angels among us.

—Don Goodman
songwriter, "Angels Among Us"

The human heart has hidden treasures…
—Charlotte Brontë

The Seven-Year-Old Hero

Little Taylor Walker had been swimming since he was six months old, and it was a good thing for a four-year-old girl that he knew his way around the water.

Taylor and his younger brother Caleb were diving and swimming in a motel pool in June the year he was seven when two little girls came to play in the pool. They splashed around and then sat at the deep end. Suddenly, one of the girls slipped into the pool and sank—she couldn't get her head above water.

"She was at the bottom of the pool when I saw her," Taylor says. "She was struggling. That's how I knew she wasn't just playing."

She wasn't coming up, either. He swam to the bottom, caught her by the arm and pulled her upward, out of danger, and brought her to the side of the pool.

Taylor's aunt, Kay Huey, was watching the children on the deck.

"There were a lot of adults and a lot of activity in the pool," she says. "No one had noticed this child had fallen in. No one but Taylor saw she was floating beneath the water's surface. He rescued her. I'm sure he saved her life."

She was so proud of him, she recommended him for awards for bravery from the American Red Cross and from the Boy Scouts.

His parents are proud of him, too.

"When you see your children do unselfish things, well, it really touches you," says his dad, John. "I'm proud of him just for being alive—he doesn't have to do a thing. He and his brother are good boys and a blessing to us." His mom, Barb, echoes him, "We are really blessed with these children."

For his part, Taylor plays down his good deed. "I knew something was happening," he says. "I didn't really think about it. I just went down there and grabbed her. It was just the right thing to do, so I did it."

For the people of Romania, Singapore, Mexico, Russia and elsewhere, there's more to the U.S. Navy than ships and patrols.

For many in the countries where ships are deployed, the troops are the source of goodwill and good works.

The Navy's Outreach Program means that wherever Navy ships go, the crew will do whatever volunteer work is needed—from painting and fixing buildings to giving school supplies to orphanages to delivering skateboards to children.

"Tears fall down my face as I am so happy for this day," wrote Mrs. Cha-on Duangkaen, in gratitude for a project in which U.S. sailors worked with a Thai community to paint two school buildings and hand out two thousand schoolbooks.

In Romania, crew members of the USS *Briscoe* spent five days at an orphanage, fixing a washing machine, replacing a window, repairing the electrical and plumbing problems and weatherproofing the playground. The sailors then had a special treat for the children—they prepared a genuine American cookout and threw a surprise birthday party for one of the kids.

But charity begins at home, too. The Memphis Naval Reserve Officer Training Corps started a new tradition last spring—the unit worked with

St. Jude Children's Research Hospital to sponsor a charity basketball tournament. An officer candidate came up with the idea when a child he knew was undergoing cancer treatment at the hospital. Basketball teams from universities all around the county and local teams from Memphis played, raising $1,000 for the battle against childhood cancer.

The tournament will be an annual event. More frequent will be the visits from NROTC volunteers, who vowed to stay in touch with the children of St. Jude's. The children who need them.

No act of kindness,
no matter how small,
is ever wasted.

—Aesop

If Wishes Were Horses

Dr. Deborah Baceski watched her daughters and other young people in her community succeed in horse shows in Somerset County, Pennsylvania. She watched them become expert in training and handling animals. But she didn't like the other side of the equestrian life—the fierce competition and judgment the children were forced to go through.

Baceski, a doctor specializing in internal medicine, wasn't the only one questioning the values the children were learning. So she and two others went to a course sponsored by the national horseback riding association. Their idea was to explore the possibility of creating a therapeutic horseback riding program for children with mental and physical handicaps. They decided to call their venture the Somerset Therapeutic Association for Riding—STAR.

Today the group meets at Baceski's property, where some forty volunteers teach riding to about two dozen children. Half of the volunteers are teens. The young people who once tried so hard to outdo one another now work together to teach their sport to others. Their concept of success has shifted. For the children they teach victory is being able to ride four laps around the ring, with two people on either side and another leading the horse.

It is a victory that fills Baceski with a sense of achievement. It fills others with awe.

Kindness is the same in any language.

Out of the Flames

Teri Macon knows her husband is a hero.

They were driving home from work in Richmond, California, one spring afternoon when they saw smoke billowing into the sky.

"I wanted to go by and see what was going on," says Teri. There were people gathered around a burning house. And confusion was everywhere. She didn't see what her husband Lorenzo was doing.

What he did scared her later, when she thought about it, but it's something she knows he'd do again in a heartbeat if he's ever in the same situation.

Lorenzo, the father of five, heard the sound of children screaming inside the burning house. He crawled through a broken window into the darkness and the smoke, and though he couldn't see, he found first one child and then another, and brought them safely outside. But someone called out that there were two more children inside, so he went back into the house. He again found first one child, then the other. He passed them through the window and climbed out of the house.

"I didn't realize it was my husband who had brought the children out of the house," says Teri. "I lost track of him—I was so concerned about the children." Soot was running down their faces, and they were coughing up black ooze. They had no clothes on, and they had to be kept warm.

She says she thinks about those kids, twin three-year-old girls, and two boys, ages seven and one, almost every day.

"I just wonder how they're doing."

I was walking ...

It was yellow ...
Then a kind ... ma...
Mama couldn't see ...
But I knew in my ...

Or I believe th...
Sent down to ...
They come to you ...
To show us ho...
To guide us ...

When life told ...
There's always been ...
A kind word from a ...
A phone call from a friend
Now ain't it kind of funn...
Someone lights the way with

With God's Help

March 27, 1994. Palm Sunday. 11:30 am.

As the tornado slammed into the side of Goshen United Methodist Church, my first thought was "Incoming!" It was like Vietnam all over again. The south side of the church collapsed, then the roof came crashing down on us. The only things saving us from being killed were the pews holding the roof off our bodies.

I remember thinking, "Are my wife, daughter and twin boys dead?" They were in the back of the church. Were they picked up by the high winds and blown away like pieces of paper? I prayed they hadn't suffered. As I lay on the floor of the church, the high winds pressed down on me. It was like being inside the sandblast booth where I work, with the nozzle turned toward me. I couldn't help my family or friends, and they couldn't help me. The only one who could help was God, and He did. The winds only lasted a few seconds. Then it became calm.

I tried to crawl out from under the roof, but I realized I was trapped. As I peeked out from underneath the pew, I saw Kelly Clem, my pastor, and a choir member throwing blocks in my direction. They were trying to uncover the children beneath the debris. Most of the children had been standing in the choir singing for the play that was being performed for the Palm Sunday service. I asked Kelly to help me, but she ignored me. I didn't realize that she was trying to find her four-year-old daughter, Hannah.

It took me five minutes to get out from under the fallen roof. When I stood, I was surprised to see a clear sky where the ceiling had been.

Then I heard sounds from under the roof and from the blocks and bricks that covered the sanctuary. There were so many people needing help that I knew this was not the time to panic. I walked slowly to keep from stepping on victims covered by the rubble. I saw a body moving under the weight of the blocks. I removed some of the debris and the woman I uncovered said, "Find my kids." I said, "I need to get you out of here, you're in the way!" By that time rescue workers were rushing in carrying stretchers. I told them to be careful where they walked, because people were under the debris. I looked around and caught a glimpse of my twin boys and daughter standing on the sidewalk. I ran over and hugged them. They told me my wife was okay and that she was checking on their Grandma Tyree. My mother was eighty-five years old and always sat with her sister, Adelle, who was ninety-six years old and the oldest member of our church.

I went to where they always sat and found them. Their bodies looked lifeless. My mother had a stick through her shoulder close to her heart. I had to break it off to be able to pick her up and hand her to a fireman. Then I turned my attention to Aunt Adelle. She was facedown on the carpet, her arm caught under a pew crushed by the fallen walls. I told her I was going to get her out of there. She said, "Go ahead and help everyone else first." I couldn't believe she said that.

Someone brought me a crowbar. I pried the bench up and slid her arm out from under it. As I picked her up I noticed that only skin was holding her dangling foot to her leg. I didn't think my mother or my aunt had much of a chance to live but I didn't have time to worry about that. I looked around for other victims. I saw a lady's leg sticking from under the edge of the roof. I told her I could pull her out but it felt like she was holding on to something. I wanted her to help push, but she said, "I can't. I'm holding on to my children." After I pulled the mother out, I pulled out all five of her children.

One of the rescue workers came up to me and suggested I go home because they had things under control. As I was leaving the church, I asked some women if everyone was out. One lady said that Janice was still inside. Janice is my sister, and as I ran over to her I could see she was trapped between two pews with the weight of a concrete beam pressing down on her. I called to her and she said, "I'm dying, I can't breathe." I used all my strength to try to lift the beam but I just couldn't. Others must have seen me because they came to help. Finally she could breathe. We used a door as a stretcher and got her to an ambulance.

The churchyard looked like a battlefield with wounded scattered around. Some people were crying, but I couldn't believe so many had actually lived. In the end, twenty people, including little Hannah, were killed and eighty-three injured. It's been almost four years now since the tornado. The church was rebuilt. This year we'll celebrate Aunt Adelle's one hundredth birthday. The people of Goshen have lived the Easter story.

—Mike Tyree
Vietnam USMC 1967-1969
Painter, combat vehicles, Anniston
Army Depot
Alabama

Great perils have this beauty, that they bring
to light the fraternity of strangers.

—Victor Hugo

In 1990, says Lieutenant Gary French, Boston was "out of control."

The Boston Police Department's commander of the Youth Violence Strike Force says the city of 600,000 was losing kids to gangs and the violence, death and injury gangs bring.

"At that time all the community agencies, the police, all the groups involved were fighting each other. Everybody was pointing the finger saying it's their fault. But we all galvanized efforts and now it's one city fighting the problem of youth violence," says French.

Among the things being done to save kids from a life—or death—of crime is Operation Cease Fire.

It's an effort that began in 1995 to save the kids who can be saved, and to lock up the ones who can't. When violence spikes in a neighborhood, all the groups, from the police to the street workers to the clergy, swing into action.

"It's a focused effort to target at-risk gang members," French explains. "We offer them options. We push them in the direction of street workers, of mentoring, of getting back into school. If they don't want to turn around, the focus rapidly turns to incarceration. We tell them if the gang violence continues, we're going to come at them with all the power we have on a city level, a state level, a federal level to take them off the street."

He calls it a carrot and a stick.

Hewitt Joyner III, 34, is on the carrot side of the equation. He's the program manager for the Boston Community Center's Street Worker Program and has been working with kids in some of the city's roughest neighborhoods since 1992.

"We do whatever it takes to get those kids on the right path," he states empatically. But he's suffered some losses.

"I just had to bury a kid. He was stabbed three times in the chest by a twenty-eight-year old," he says. His voice is somber. "He was just in the wrong place at the wrong time. He was a good kid."

Joyner sees all kids as having it in them to be good. He remembers one thirteen-year-old he met who was tearing up a classroom, wild and out of control. Today that boy has given up gang life for a chance to learn a trade.

"We just try to keep them busy and keep pounding information into their heads. When we see them do something, we check them on it. These kids love structure, and the harder a kid is the more I love him. I might lose a few, but if I lose one I gain ten."

He says he and his co-workers give the kids the tools they need. If a kid can't get a job because he can't read, they get him into a reading program. If he has no skills, they find job training.

Are gang members listening? The people involved in Cease Fire think so. Boston's violent crime rate is at a thirty or forty-year low, its homicides have dropped from 160 in 1990 to the low forties this year.

Reverend Zina Jacque, a minister at the Union Baptist Church in Cambridge is also part of the Operation Cease Fire experiment. She's seen the proof, too.

"One young man was very much in the life, selling drugs, and now he's applying to law school," she says. One of the ministers working on the streets helped the young man, touched him. "He has a little girl and he decided he wanted something different for his daughter than a dead father."

Gun Denhart wanted a way to show the world the colorful children's clothes she manufactured would stand the test of time. She wanted to show they were so well made, it would take more than one kid to wear them out.

She and her husband Tom are cofounders of Hanna Andersson, a mail-order children's wear firm based in Portland, Oregon. Since 1984, the company has invited customers to send back outgrown outfits in return for a twenty-percent credit on their next purchase. The clothing is then donated to needy families throughout the U.S. Last year, more than 133,000 "Hannadowns" were distributed to children who needed them.

"We had no idea where it would lead," said Gun. "I grew up in Sweden, where things are very different. This has opened my eyes to how many children go without clothing. It tears my heart apart."

She can't give the children everything they need to feel safe in the world. But she can give them warm clothes to wear.

Love sought is good, but given unsought is better.

—William Shakespeare

Pamela Silver heard the song for the first time when she was living in a Manhattan nursing home. She wanted to listen to it over and over again. It wasn't played on the radio. It was her song, written just for her.

"A girl who never had a smile on her face had a grin from ear to ear," says her mom, Regina Silver-Koplo. "It was incredible."

Pamela was diagnosed with Huntington's disease when she was twenty-two years old. Her mother had noticed her depression, her mood swings, her occasional clumsiness but chalked it up to the trauma of her parents' divorce, or maybe just the by-product of growing up. The bright, popular and pretty young woman slowly slipped into the clutches of the disease, which has robbed her of motor skills, but not her quick mind.

Her mother heard about Songs of Love, an organization devoted to creating songs for and about ill children. Although she thought her twenty-nine-year-old daughter would be too old, she sent some information about Pamela anyway, and the people at Songs of Love called back for more. Regina told the songwriter about how inside her daughter's body was a functioning mind, about Poochie, the cat Pamela rescued when she was eighteen, and about her family. Then one day the tape came in the mail.

"The first time I played it for her, it was incredible. She has chorea, which is involuntary shaking movements. When I played the song her body went totally still. There was a smile on her face, and I could see she was really listening, listening intently," says Regina. "I asked her if she wanted to hear it again, and I could see the tears streaming down her face. I played it over and over for her, and I play it for her every time I see her."

Songs of Love was started by John Beltzer, a songwriter living in Queens, New York, who had fallen on hard times back in 1995. A record deal fell apart, his relationship with his girlfriend crumbled. Beltzer says he was walking down the street one day and the idea hit him with the force of a revelation—he'd written songs for people before, why not write them for ill children? He called St. Jude Children's Research Hospital in Memphis and received information about six children. He wrote six songs in four days, and the response was overwhelming.

Beltzer knows now the race for a record deal is no longer what music is for him. "It's about stepping out of the sphere of ego into the sphere of compassion," he says. Today there are more than 130 songwriters across America who have written music for more than 600 sick children.

The music has power to soothe them, to make them smile.

A song had the power to bring joy to Pamela. "The song says, 'We know who you are,'" notes her mom. "It says, 'You're not alone.'"

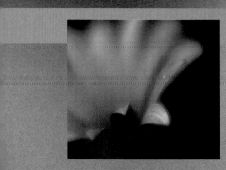

Mattie Dotson was the youngest of her mother's ten children and the only one to be abandoned by her. It was a hurt she will never forget.

When four of her five children grew up and moved away, Dotson wanted to fill the house up again. She opened her home and her heart to children who were not loved well by those who should love them most. Dotson became a foster parent. She wanted to help children since, as she says, "I can feel the way they're feeling."

In the past ten years, Dotson has been mama to more than fifty children. They enter her house as so-called problem children, but she doesn't see it that way. What she sees are children who are angry, disappointed, hurt.

The first boy she took in was like that. "He didn't know what was going to happen to him, and he acted the only way he knew to act, by cutting up and cussing." She told him if he really didn't want to stay she would call his social worker in the morning and he could leave. But as the night wore on, they talked. By morning, he asked if he could stay. He stayed four years, finished high school, and now has a good job.

Mattie Dotson has a few rules. There is to be respect for all people. No one will be mistreated. No one will be abandoned if they do wrong. There will be comfort when there is sadness. There will be someone to stick up for them at school. There will be someone to listen to their side. There will be love.

The children all come to her house scared that she will want to take the place of their mothers, but she never does. She makes sure they know that, for now, their parents can't look after them so she will. She makes sure the children have gifts for their parents at Christmas, and on their birthdays, and on Mother's and Father's Day. She tells them that no matter what, they can make a life for themselves and then they can go back and help their parents if their parents can't help themselves.

"Even though I tell them I love them, they still want their mothers. They still have that yearning and longing. I recognize that," Dotson says. "I felt that."

She says she will be what they all come to call her in their own time—Mama—until the day she dies. "I want them to grow up and make something of themselves. I want to just wipe the pain away. To see them being happy, just to see a little bitty smile— that makes my day."

For the children, it makes their lives.

Miles Postlethwait of Lenexa, Kansas, was six years old and home from school back in 1993. He wasn't home with something as simple as a stomach ache—he was born with congenital heart and intestinal defects, and he'd had twenty-nine surgeries already. He was home because his colostomy was acting up and he would probably need more medical procedures.

"He was having a really bad day, and we were getting ready to go to the hospital for more tests. He looked up at me and said, 'I wish I had a friend just like me,'" his mother Marty remembers. "I told him, 'You do,' and I started naming his friends in the neighborhood. He said, 'No Mom, I mean just like me, with an incision and a colostomy.' He also said all his toys were perfect. I thought to myself, 'You know, he's right.'"

Marty started thinking about how to give her son a friend that would really comfort him.

"I used to work in an operating room as a scheduler and I saw how scared those children would be. I started researching into comforting educational tools given to children, and I found there was nothing that a child could actually keep once he bonded with it. So Miles and I sat down and created Shadow Buddies."

Shadow Buddies are soft muslin dolls designed with the same incisions and marks and equipment sick kids have. They are pals to seriously ill children who have to go through scary medical procedures, and take their name from the song, "Me and My Shadow."

Marty and Miles started with four Buddies, and now there are seventeen—Buddies without hair, which are given to children undergoing cancer treatment, Buddies with upside-down Y-shaped incisions for children with liver transplants, a Buddy with an inhaler for children with respiratory problems like asthma. There's even an HIV-positive Buddy, with pinpricks to show where blood tests have been done and a big red ribbon on its hospital gown.

The Shadow Buddies are distributed through hospitals all over the U.S. and parts of Canada, and their cost—about ten dollars each—is usually picked up by corporate sponsorship.

Marty is now working on the Shadow Buddy Foundation, which will distribute hundreds of Buddies to hospitals that can't afford them.

"The children all relate to their buddy. I once visited a three-year-old with cancer, and I asked him what he wanted. He said, 'I want a happy face just like my Buddy,'" says Marty.

"Usually I have one good cry a day. At least I know I'm helping."

Helen ver Duin Palit's mother told her never to waste a thing, especially food. Palit took those words to heart.

Today, she runs Angel Harvest, an organization that picks up the sumptuous leftovers from celebrity parties and brings it to soup kitchens, shelters, drug and alcohol rehabilitation centers, seniors and AIDS programs and day care centres. There, hungry people eat good food including seafood, grilled chicken in red corn tacos, andouille sausage—nourishment that otherwise would go to waste.

"Los Angeles is an incredible place. The parties are huge—I was once at a party for nineteen thousand people. There are towns in Canada and the U.S. smaller than that. Caterers here tell us they make

...When I give I give myself.
—Walt Whitman

more food per person than they do elsewhere. And there are more people on a diet here than anywhere else—for our business, it's great!" Palit says.

Angel Harvest is only her latest venture into feeding the hungry. Palit hit upon the idea while running a soup kitchen for Yale University in 1980.

"One day was particularly trying and I attempted to wind down at a restaurant next door. We were eating potato skins, and I thought, 'What do they do with the insides?'" The next day, and most days after that, the soup kitchen was given thirty gallons of potatoes.

"Our soup was now potato chowder," she laughs. "A couple of weeks later the restaurant brought over twelve quiches—the special was ham-and-cheese quiche and the chef had forgotten to put in the ham. I quickly realized there were a lot of companies that had food, and everybody periodically had leftovers."

In 1982 she moved to New York City and looked around for a similar program. There was none. So she did her homework and developed City Harvest, an organization that picks up and distributes perishable food from restaurants, parties and corporate boardrooms, to name just a few of her sources. Today, City Harvest delivers more than 20,000 meals a day to those in need. From there Palit created America Harvest, which helps other cities establish programs to turn leftovers into meals for the hungry.

So far, because of Palit's idea and her desire not to waste food as long as people go without, there are 120 such programs in the U.S., and eighty-five in Canada and Germany. All over the world, the Harvest programs provide food for over 300,000 meals a day.

Not all of it is andouille and seafood. But it's all good food.

There weren't many people who could make little Andy Bremner's day like the mailman.

Andy was eight when he was diagnosed with non-Hodgkin's lymphoma. His mother Linda remembers how he would be lying on the living room couch, grumpy with pain and too tired to play or talk or read a book. But when the mailman showed up, Andy's face would light up and he would run to the door just to see what he'd brought.

When Andy went into the hospital the first time, dozens of friends and relatives sent him mail, and sometimes he would even take his cards and letters right into bed with him. But when he went home again, the mail dropped off. It's not that people don't care, his mother says. It's that they don't know what to say. You can't write "Get well soon" to a boy who won't. But Andy's mother knew how much it meant to him, so she devised a plan. She wrote to her son every day and signed her letters, "Your Secret Pal."

One day she found him drawing a picture at the dining room table. He said it was a special gift for his secret friend. He signed it, "P.S.: Mom, I love you." Andy knew who his secret friend really was but it didn't matter. His mother still wrote to him every day. It was her chance to say "I love you" back.

Andy lost his fight with cancer in 1984. After he died, his mom found a box full of her letters to her son, with an address book filled with the names of the friends he'd made at camp for children with cancer. She remembered how Andy would look forward to that special time when the mailman came. She sat down and started writing letters to every child whose name Andy had written in his book. Before she'd finished, she received a reply. A twelve-year-old boy wrote to thank her for writing. "I didn't know anyone knew I lived," he wrote.

"It knocked my socks off!" Linda says. "I never knew other kids felt the way Andy did." That's when she knew what she had to do.

Today Love Letters, based in Lombard, Ill., is a group of seventy volunteers who write cheery cards and letters every week to more than 1,100 seriously ill children all over America. On their birthdays, the children receive extra things in the mail—a birthday note, a handmade card, and a gift from their special friend. "We're in the smile business," Andy's mom says. Smiles that come with the mail.

The Good Fight

Harry Watkins says it was war that made him think about his hometown in a new way. He came back from the Persian Gulf and declared war himself—on the poverty, the drugs and the lack of hope he saw in the city where he grew up.

Watkins and his wife, Leslyne, both registered nurses and parents of three sons, had been involved in community work for more than a decade in Lebanon, Tennessee. It's a small city thirty miles east of Nashville, but it had some big-city problems. Kids were getting into drugs and staying there. Violence was escalating and people didn't have adequate housing. The Watkinses and some like-minded colleagues started the Wilson County Civic League to fight the housing problem, the illiteracy and the drugs.

Not long after Watkins returned from the Gulf, they mobilized. The group started building connections with church and community leaders to lobby to take over a dilapidated school abandoned after desegregation made it redundant. Harry realized that to really build a community, the community needed a home.

"I came back from the Gulf in 1991 and I saw this desperate need. I came back stronger. I realized there was so much more I wanted to do," says Harry. "I saw that if we could somehow get that old building we could get these young people off the streets and into recreation and tutoring programs."

The group had to lobby hard. But in 1993, it acquired the school, which had become a hangout for drug dealers, for five dollars. With $200,000 in contributions and grants for repairs and the help of people in the neighborhood who donated their time and energy, the school was transformed into the hub of the community.

Today, the kids who used to throw rocks at the windows are inside playing basketball, improving their reading and math skills and listening to athletes and community leaders talk about the way out of the ghetto and the rewards of hard work. And local police report that drug use is down as much as fifty percent, violence has decreased and kids are staying in school.

"I know we're touching these kids," says Watkins.

Leslyne recalls a little girl who started coming to the center when it opened. She's in fifth grade now, and sometimes helps teach the kindergarten kids their ABC's and 1-2-3's.

"She says she wants to be a teacher. To see her enthusiasm, to watch her develop and now to see her reaching back to help other little girls, that was joy to me."

A hero is a man who does what he can.

—Romain Rolland

The Rescue

Fred Puleo says he's not as religious as some. But when he thinks back to a freak snowstorm in Texas and the strange events that led him to save the lives of two little girls, he believes God's hand was at work.

When he talks about it, he likes to start the story several hours earlier. He and his co-workers were in Dallas, at a U.S. government-sponsored workshop for nuclear power workers. As the conference wound down, the weather turned ugly—a cold front blew in, what people in Texas call "Blue Northers." Puleo's group decided not to chance the airport, which they expected to close due to the weather anyway. They were anxious to get back to their families and chose instead to drive to Bay City, their hometown on the coast.

As they drove, a tractor trailer sped by. "We said we'd see that one in the ditch and sure enough, a few miles ahead we saw it had jackknifed and was wedged into a bridge." Their route was cut off.

Puleo and his passengers turned back and asked directions for another way home. They headed off on another highway, but were warned about a bridge over a reservoir that could be treacherous in the storm.

"We saw the bridge…. Then we saw the pickup ahead of us just stop. At first we couldn't see past him, but then I saw a car perpendicular to the concrete wall at the bridge. The car was just embedded," said Puleo. Puleo stopped his car and ran to see if he could help. The accident was much worse than it had looked. An elderly woman was in the driver's seat, her color "dreadful." He thought she was dead. Then Puleo heard a tiny voice in the back seat saying, "Mister, can you help me?"

"I jumped in the back seat and the little girl said, 'Mister, I think I broke my arm,'" said Puleo. "I could see the outline of her bone pushing the skin in her wrist. I said, 'Yeah honey, I think you broke your arm.' She said, 'I think I broke my leg, too,' and I could see the outline of the bone through her pants."

The little girl was frightened and in shock, and Puleo made her as comfortable as he could. She begged him not to leave her.

"Smoke started coming out from the engine. I stood on the door frame and called to other drivers to call for help, a little girl was hurt."

As he did so, a man poked his head in the open front passenger window. Puleo asked him to please keep an eye on the smoke, because if it turned to flame he'd have to move the child, which he didn't want to do if he didn't need to.

"Then we heard this little shrill squeaky noise and our eyes met and I thought, Oh my God, there's somebody else in the car."

The front passenger seat was crumpled over, so Puleo felt for another passenger. Wedged up under the dashboard was another little girl. Just as they found her, flames shot up from the engine. The other man, Norman Guy of Mesquite, Texas, frantically tried to open the door, and Puleo kicked it from the back seat. It popped open, but the two men couldn't push the child out—her seat belt was still on.

"I said we need a knife and he ran and got a knife," said Puleo. The flames started to roll, and he carried the first child to the side of the road. Together the two men managed to extricate the tiny one caught in the front seat. As Puleo ran with her, he saw her socks and shoes were on fire. He put her down and threw them off, just as the car became engulfed in flames.

Although they couldn't save the elderly driver, the two little girls recovered. When Puleo thinks back, he believes the odd happenings—the strange weather, the jackknifed trailer, the alternate route, the tiny sound an unconscious girl made— were all a pattern, so that he and the stranger who poked his head in the window could save the two little girls.

"I believe we were meant to be there," says Puleo. "I believe God does work in mysterious ways."

Those Who Can...Teach

For eight minutes on October 18, 1993, Caroline Borum's sixth grade students from Sycamore Middle School were in contact with the universe.

With sponsorship from Bob Jewell and State Industries, Borum applied to a special NASA SAREX project that connects astronauts in space with students via radio. When Borum got word that her school had been selected to speak to the crew of the space shuttle *Columbia*, there were just eight weeks to get the students trained and ready to make contact.

"We brought in equipment and we decided to make the contact manually. We had twelve students work out the coordinates and set the antennae," said Borum, who teaches in Cheatham County, a rural community about twenty miles north of Nashville. The children had to use computer programs to track the space shuttle. They learned about azimuth and elevation antennae and had to move their antennae one tenth of a wavelength so that the twelve-inch antennae on the shuttle could rescue their messages. The easy alternative would have been to send a radio message to a satellite link—with a guaranteed one hundred percent success rate—but Borum thought her students would learn much more if they did it manually.

"It was almost impossible. Some of the kids had never touched a computer at all, and we could only train an hour a day."

To involve more students, Borum organized a contest among the ten schools in the county. Children entered questions they wanted to ask the astronauts, and the governor visited the school and randomly selected ten questions.

As the time drew near, Borum's students practiced asking the questions over a radio, so that they would be efficient enough to ask all ten in the eight minutes they would have when the shuttle was in range.

Since the shuttle was on a medical mission and would be carrying laboratory rats, Borum got even more students involved by setting up some testing on mice in her classroom, creating experiments on nutrition.

At 1:15 p.m. on October 18, the students made contact with the astronauts. They asked their questions and heard the answers clear as could be. The school gym was crammed with parents, students and media who watched pictures of the shuttle on a huge TV screen while the astronauts talked.

"It's a miracle we were able to do it," Borum exclaimed. She said college students were also trying to make contact, but failed. "Here were these kids who had just finished the sixth grade doing it manually."

Today, the fascination with space continues. Each year the county holds a space science competition for students, and the winners go to the U.S. Space and Rocket Center in Huntsville, Alabama, where they can tour the base, see astronauts train, check out space shuttles and even get a taste of life in space through a virtual reality program.

As for Borum, she's trying to get the funding to set up robotics experiments for her class, so her students can build robots and test their own limits.

"I feel that as a teacher, you have to be enthusiastic," said Borum. "The students catch that spirit."

Peter Westbrook believes he's lived by the sword.

"I was an inner city kid and if not for fencing I would be like everyone else I grew up with—ninety percent are dead and ten percent are incarcerated or on drugs." Westbrook, a six-time Olympian who grew up the son of a Japanese mother and a Black father in the projects of Newark, New Jersey, says, "Fencing saved my life."

His parents split up when he was three years old, and he says the other kids used to make fun of him for his mixed ancestry, his absent father, his poverty.

But Westbrook escaped by becoming not just a fencer, but a champion. He won bronze in the 1984 Olympic Games in Los Angeles, making him the first American fencer to win an Olympic medal in twenty-four years. Now, he wants to give something back.

First, he gave money to those on the streets. "One man I saw needed shoes so I bought him some. Once I gave this lady five dollars and she put it on the floor—she was so out of it. I realized that when you give money, it might not be used properly," he says. So he decided to give back exactly what he took—lessons and guidance and coaching in the sport of kings.

Every Saturday for the past seven years, the Peter Westbrook Foundation draws dozens of disadvantaged kids from Harlem, the Bronx, Queens and elsewhere to Manhattan's New York Fencers Club. Everything they need is there: the equipment, the world-caliber coaches, the love, the support. There's also a tutoring program, and every month doctors, lawyers, surgeons and other professionals come in and speak to the children, too, so they can see the possibilities the world holds for them.

"We run a tight ship," says Westbrook, who has spent thousands of dollars of his own to start the foundation. "We are highly disciplined. But the kids can see how much love there is, too."

For the past four years, the youth of the foundation have competed for the U.S.A. in junior and senior world championships and in July 1997, his kids won national fencing championships in Colorado.

But the kids win more than sporting events. They win self-respect, they learn discipline, and they earn a ticket out of hardship.

She had just come out of the shower when she heard the screaming.

Dana Loraine Goodge grabbed a robe, told her youngest daughter to stay put on the living room couch and ran out the front door to see what was the matter.

Her eldest daughter came running toward her screaming. Behind her Goodge could see two dogs ripping at a little girl as if she were a doll.

"I told my daughter to go in the house and I saw people standing around watching. I just ran and picked up one of the dogs and threw him across the street."

The nine-year-old had been walking toward the school bus in Tuscon, Arizona, in August 1996, when the dogs started nipping at her. The more afraid she became the more aggressive the dogs were, biting at her backpack and her long braid, then mauling her.

"I realized the dogs weren't biting me, they were only after her so I knew I had to lie on her to protect her," Goodge explained. One of the dogs bit her and "the pain was so excruciating I had to roll over, and I was screaming at the people to do something."

Two men jumped out of their truck and distracted the dogs long enough for Goodge to run to her home holding the child. Her daughter was on the phone to 911. Goodge wrapped the little girl in a coverlet and waited for the ambulance.

When she went to the hospital a short time later, Goodge was able to see the child, though she was strapped to a trauma board.

"I said, 'Hi sweetie,' and she said, 'thank you for saving my life,'" said Goodge. "She told me she loved me, and that's when it hit me the hardest. I was just overcome. I told her I had to go so they could take care of her.

"When I left I was crying and her family was hugging me. I felt it was God who was holding me."

Goodge believes that if she'd stayed in the shower "even two more minutes she would have been dead." What frightens her even now is that no one else seemed to be doing anything to save the little girl.

"I've struggled my whole life and I always wanted to be able to help someone like me up the ladder," Goodge added. She's grateful she got a chance.

Since the attack, she's kept in touch with the child.

"She's just a beautiful little girl."

Lucille Williams looked fine for someone whose vehicle had been hit head-on by a drunk driver on a country highway in Tennessee. She was able to wander about the scene of the crash and say a few words.

When the emergency medical team arrived, thick fog had settled in and the scene was chaotic. Three vehicles were involved, one of them an eighteen-wheel transport. Lucille, then seventy, had been traveling with two friends on her way home from square dancing and appeared to suffer only an open fracture to her wrist. Derek Crow and Dana Bradberry strapped her onto the spinal board and lifted her into the ambulance to take her several miles away to an orthopedic hospital.

Then things took a drastic turn.

"In a matter of three minutes her head swelled

to the size of a basketball. There was blood coming from her eyes, her ears...and her mouth started to swell shut," says Crow. He grabbed a suction catheter, not what he would normally use but the only thing small enough to get through her swelling throat, to create an airway. "It was almost like lying in that position on the board caused the blood to rush to her head and she went critical."

Crow called to Bradberry to turn around and head back to the closest hospital. Their patient was in trouble. Bradberry raced through the fog—Crow says he doesn't know how she did it—to get their patient to the hospital where an emergency tracheotomy saved her life.

"This case was the strangest one because she didn't appear to have any injuries. She was the least critical at the scene, and if we'd had only one ambulance, she would have been sitting on the side of the road until everyone else had been transported," notes Crow. "It just shows how quickly an accident can shift."

Bradberry never saw Lucille again, but by happenstance she ran into her granddaughter one Mother's Day weekend, a few years after the accident.

"Her granddaughter thanked me for the fact her grandmother was still alive," says Bradberry. "I told her to give her my love and tell her I think of her often."

"This job changes you. You are dealing with people's lives, and you have to respect that. This job makes you respect life."

When Habitat for Humanity told Pat and Gerald Turner they'd be getting a new home, it was like a dream come true.

For a long time they'd wanted to move out of their cramped two-bedroom apartment, which they shared with their two young sons and Gerald's mother. They were thrilled to learn that the Blessed Sacrament Catholic Community had agreed to work in partnership with Habitat—which has built homes for more than fifty thousand families around the world since 1976—to build the house to be located on North Patrick Street in Old Town, the historic section of Alexandria, Virginia.

Volunteers from the parish, who took on the project to celebrate the parish's fifty-year jubilee and dubbed the house Jubilee House, worked hard from May to July. Gerald Turner was out there, too, helping to build his family's home.

On Sunday, July 28, 1996, the Turners and the workers got devastating news. Fire, believed to be arson, had destroyed everything.

"Sad—that's exactly how people felt, and disappointed, and maybe even hurt and a little bit angry," says Anne Murphy, who, with Ken Naser headed the project. "But a lot of good things came out of that fire." The volunteers, the Turners and others who heard about the blaze said a prayer over the ashes. Then they got to work. A two-week blitz restored all the work done before the fire and more. People who'd been lukewarm about the project pitched in with their whole hearts. In October, the Turner family moved in.

"When I first heard about the fire, I was in shock and disbelief," reveals Gerald. "I went into denial—we had worked so hard, and so many other people had worked so hard. We prayed, and the people from Blessed Sacrament were right there for us—we all cried together. Then it's like everybody made up their minds this house was going to be done."

That effort for his family meant a lot to him. Gerald had been addicted to drugs and alcohol for twenty-four years and had learned to trust no one. "I never thought I could accomplish anything or have anything. I've been clean four years, and as soon as I got clean the little blessings started coming."

He says the volunteers taught him to trust people, and to trust their good intentions.

"These people gave and gave freely," he says. "We love those people, and they're still our friends." He now works on other houses for Habitat, sharing the goodwill he received.

"It was beautiful to watch how everything came together for us. It's the miracle on North Patrick Street."

Good Neighbors

Lawrence Maiello was a man who kept to himself. But when he was in trouble, the people of the small town of Walker Valley, New York, banded together to help him. He was their neighbor, and being a neighbor means something to them.

The Ennists had always kept an eye out for the elderly man who lived in a mobile home behind their house, doing little things for him like turning off his car lights when he left them on—things Maiello didn't even seem to notice. Timothy Carroll knew Maiello liked his privacy, but he'd help him out, too, by fixing his lawn mower when it broke and clearing his driveway.

But in February, 1996, Maiello needed everyone's help. One night, Patricia Ennist looked out her window and saw smoke billowing from his tiny trailer. Her husband Percy, who had been a volunteer firefighter in a nearby town for thirty years, ran over to make sure the elderly man had gotten out. "I hollered for him and I barely heard his voice inside. I broke down the front door," says Percy.

Flames shot fifteen to twenty feet in the air. In spite of the flames, the smoke, the intense heat, Percy ran inside. "There was smoke three feet off the floor. But I knew about where he would be, and I went over there. I found him crouched in the corner." He picked up the eighty-five-year-old man and threw him over his shoulder, managing to get him out of there. The trailer, though, was finished.

According to Carroll, "People heard about that and they started coming out, giving five-dollar or ten-dollar donations, whatever they had, to help him." Carroll decided that the old man who reminded him of his own father had to have his home back.

"His whole life had been that ten-by-thirty-foot trailer."

He tore down the ruined trailer, and the town's scrap collector donated his time and energy to take the wreckage away. There was $2,000 hidden in the floorboards, and that was used to buy another mobile home. Carroll poured new footings and put in another gravel driveway. Other volunteers came out to help build a porch, to paint, to put in the plumbing and electricity. "Everybody pitched in to do what they had to do for him," says Carroll.

When Maiello came back to his new home, "He was just ecstatic," Carroll remembers. "You should've seen the smile on his face. He said 'Oh, buddy, you don't know what you've done for me' but I told him it was very little compared to the satisfaction we got."

Maiello stayed in his new home just one day before his health took another turn. He died not long after.

"He was so happy," says Carroll. That one day and all it meant was worth it.

Let all your things be done with charity.
—1 Corinthians 16:14

...ale Marie Clark's life hard. But she transformed her grief and her pain
... hope for other people.

...husband Thomas died in a sawmill accident in May 1989, her world and
...her two sons "turned upside down." Ten weeks later, when her older son
...was killed in a fiery car crash, she was in paralyzing shock, barely able to
...for two solid days.

..."a lot from the people who came forward to help us," Clark states, and she
...had tremendous support from her family, friends and neighbors in
Mt. Vernon, Maine. "My mother and dad were an inspiration. We knew we needed
to do something positive."

The first thing she did was establish an annual scholarship, to be given to high
school students in her son's and husband's memory. Four years later she felt strong
enough to take a step she'd been thinking about for a long time. Clark, a nurse, got
involved in Maine's hospice programs. She worked with the Grieving Children
Program in Augusta for a year. She now heads the bereavement program for the
Hospice Volunteers of Waterville, to help families cope with loss.

"For four years my son Matthew and I did some healthy grieving," she reveals. "We
got to know each other. We talked together, we cried together…but in about four years
I felt strong enough, I knew I could go out there and help other people who were in
pain."

It was her idea as the bereavement coordinator to get to work on creating an annual
weekend retreat, a camp where stricken families could go to be with each other and to

learn to see death as part of the cycle of nature and their pain as part of the process.

She came up with the name for the camp the night she said goodbye to the families she helped in the Grieving Children Program. With her new commitments at work and to her family, she felt she could no longer continue. "I was so sad about that—I had come to love the families I was working with, and on the last night my heart felt very heavy," she says.

She struggled with how to say goodbye. As she pulled into a parking spot, with her hand on the key to turn off the ignition, she heard "Angels Among Us" for the first time. A line from the song—"Someone lights the way with just a single ray of hope"— struck her like a shock wave. Ray of Hope, she knew, would be the name of the camp she wanted to start.

There have been three annual retreats since then. In September 1997 she added a few new things to Camp Ray of Hope. There was a ceremony around a spruce tree planted in a small clearing when the camp began. Families hung ornaments made from pinecones, moss—whatever nature gave them—and said a tribute to their loved ones. It's a ceremony, Clark says, that holds the lesson that "all things return to nature, just as people do." This year the families also set free monarch butterflies, which in the fall begin their journey to Mexico, where the Aztecs once believed them to be the spirits of fallen heroes.

"Doing this work makes me feel I have taken my life experience and funneled it into avenues where it is really going to make a difference to others," says Clark. "I feel I have two angels sitting on my shoulders, guiding me."

Look up and not down,
look out and not in,
look forward and not back,
and lend a hand.

—Edward Everett Hale

Angels I Know